Horse Behaviour Explained

Horse Behaviour Explained

Behavioural Science for Riders

Angelika Schmelzer

Copyright of original edition © 2002
by Cadmos Verlag GmbH, Brunsbek
Copyright of this edition © 2003 by Cadmos Equestrian
Translated by Ute Weyer MRCVS
Layout: Ravenstein + Partner, Verden
Photographs: Angelika Schmelzer
Print and Binding: Proost, Turnhout

ISBN 3-86127-909-6

Contents

Behavioural science

1

Behavioural science or behavioural research, otherwise termed "ethology", deals with the laws of animal behaviour. The word ethology stems from the old Greek words "ethos" (custom, habit) and "logos" (science). Ethology is a relatively new area of science, but has certainly caught the interest of many animal lovers over the last few years.

The reason why

For around 100 years scientists have been trying to understand the laws of animal behaviour.

They have focused on detecting causes, describing processes and accurately predicting behaviour. A clearer understanding of the behaviour of domestic animals can be gained from research on wild animals. Researchers are also interested in domestic animals, not least because people are using animals more and more, both professionally and as a rewarding, relaxing hobby. Historically, animals were often

treated as mere objects, or were "humanised". Behavioural research now enables us to have a better understanding and appreciation of typical "animalistic" qualities.

We horse lovers often ask "why", especially when we notice or dislike a particular aspect of the behaviour of our four-legged friends: why does my horse not behave the same all the time, why is it suddenly not like it was before, or why is it somehow different from its companions?

"Problem horses" in a wider sense are often the reason for more developing interest in behavioural studies: the more frustrating our experience with the problem horse, the greater our interest in causes, prevention and solutions.

One further incentive for being curious derives from the teaching techniques of popular trainers. Their various methods of training, education or correction are, despite all their differences, based on insight into the natural behaviour of horses, and communication between horse and human – sometimes

The various playful techniques used in free dressage are all based on communication between species.

transparent and scientific, sometimes not.

To separate the good methods from the bad, one needs a well-developed knowledge of equine behaviour in general, and horse language in particular. Only with this knowledge, which cannot be picked up at a weekend course, can these methods be used in a sensible and beneficial way.

In any case, most riders are interested in the psyche of their horses

because the early stages of behavioural research have, along with other factors, triggered significant changes in equine sports, which are of great consequence.

Insight into horses' natural behaviour and their specific requirements has led to more and more horses being kept in species-specific conditions which give riders and breeders the opportunity to watch their animals displaying their natural manners.

Two stallions meet:
how will they react?
And why?

The causes of behaviour

Behavioural research explores many paths, but the basis of the science is to find laws.

Animal behaviour is, of course, not predictable, unlike that of a machine that carries out the same mechanical event on pressing a button. Nevertheless, causes for certain behaviour can be detected and defined, and predictions can be made. For the horse lover, the following starting points are of particular interest:

- What is a horse's "normal" behaviour?
- How do I have to keep, feed and work my horse so that it shows "normal" behaviour?
- How are behavioural patterns that would be called "abnormal" evoked?
- How can I avoid these patterns?
- If certain aspects of behaviour are inherited, does this also apply for "abnormal" behaviour?

Species-specific behaviour is partly genetic, partly environmental.

Horse lovers - not incorrectly - associate normal behaviour with well being and connect a lack of well being with deviations from this rule. This leads to the following associations:

Horse owner's knowledge of requirements and typical behaviour of their horses

↓

Designing the environment in order to provide stabling, training and education appropriate for the equine species

↓

Displaying species-specific behavioural patterns

↓

Maximum wellbeing of the horse, together with longevity, health and good performance

What is normal?

Sometimes, what seems so obvious at first glance can prove to be less clear-cut in practice.

We are used to thinking of an animal's behaviour as "normal" or "abnormal", and often forget that each human influence has to be understood as manipulation and that it affects a horse's conduct in a way that is neither normal nor natural. We horse lovers are therefore forced to perform a fine balancing act.

The yard-stick is on the one hand the behaviour of the wild horse, and

on the other the behaviour of a comparable, but domesticated horse. That is not the only difficulty, because the casual use of the expression "problem horse" leads to confusion as well.

We often tend to throw unwanted behaviour and behavioural disturbances into one pot simply because we do not want either of them to happen. As behavioural researchers of the future, however, we should distinguish precisely whether we are dealing with a deviation from a norm, or rather with a natural pattern, expressed in a way that causes a problem for us.

We should always bear in mind that our influence on a horse is not strictly natural, and that every contact with humans has to be managed in such a way that a horse can remain a horse. True love of horses will be measured against that!

2 Behind the scenes in the **horse family**

Looking at the various horse breeds in the world, we notice big differences in their conformation.

If we did not know better, these variations would make us question whether the miniature Shetland, Shire horse, Icelandic pony and Arabian horse all belong to the same species.

Looking closer still, we notice other significant differences, for instance in their behaviour and gaits. Even horses of the same breed are not identical and can show very different characteristics.

Despite this, the common features of all individuals and breeds are such that we can identify more similarities than differences, separating horses from other species.

Wild animals in the stable

While the horse's ancestors looked very similar to each other, the domesticated horse shows a great variation in conformation. This could lead us to believe that the internal make up of a horse is influenced and changed by domestication in the same way as their exterior. The fact that many behavioural patterns are not expressed under unnatural conditions is often misunderstood. Nevertheless, we can state that:

• Our domesticated horse breeds do not show significantly different behavioural patterns than their ancestors or any living wild horses.

• Even amongst different breeds the basic behavioural structure remains the same.

Under similar conditions, a Shetland pony will react in the same way as a Shire horse, a mustang, or a Przewalski horse.

An inventory for the horse family

In order to gain insight into the typical behaviour of a species, scientists first have to list all the identified behavioural characteristics.

It is important to distinguish between behavioural patterns commonly displayed by all members of

This response is known as "flehming" – the stallion is scenting a mare in season.

a species, and possible deviations of individuals or groups. Such an "inventory" list is called an ethogram, in which all behavioural patterns that serve the same purpose are assigned to the same functional group.

Not without my companion!

Even the non-scientific horse lover has to gain experience with horses that behave in a normal way, to be able to develop a yardstick. Only under certain circumstances is it

Basic requirements of all horses: light, air, exercise and company.

possible to study the whole spectrum of behaviour.

This is easiest to observe under conditions that are similar to those of the wild ancestors of our horses, or at least amongst naturally and properly kept animals.

The more the horse's natural requirements are fulfilled, the more fully will its natural behavioural patterns be expressed; vice versa, the full expression of natural behaviour can be seen as an indicator of correct stable management.

It is of utmost importance to keep horses in a group, because they are herd animals. Without their com-

panions, not only is social behaviour missing, but also other functions will not be expressed normally.

Appropriate stable management must satisfy the following basic requirements:
• constant companionship
• free movement
• fresh air and
• natural light.

Horses are both flight and herd animals, and therefore require certain living conditions in order to be able to behave normally. Only then can their genetic inventory be displayed and observed.

The **natural order**

Back to the question: what is normal for horses? Normality is life in a community, life that is determined by hierarchy and a variety of rules and habits. Being a flight animal, the horse requires a regulated structure to feel safe and well and to be able to relax.

The social structure

We generally speak about horse herds, but the social life of horses takes place in smaller units - family groups. These family groups consist of:
• the dominant female, usually an older, experienced mare...
• her female offspring...
• female and male offspring of other mares, the males not older than two years, and
• the dominant stallion or harem's stallion.

The "leading stallion", an expression so frequently used in liter-

The watchful wild stallion protects his mares from the unknown visitor.

ature, does not really exist in nature. The herd is led by a dominant mare; stallions don't lead the herd, they drive it. The horse family shares the roles of its members in a way that has nothing to do with the human understanding of role behaviour.

The task of the leading mare, an older, experienced (you could say "wise") mare, is to guide the herd to water, feeding areas and resting places. Her leading role is connected with certain duties, some risks and of course privileges. One of her responsibilities is checking out possible dangers.

As the mare is the first one to eat and drink, and arrives before the others, she automatically inspects the environment and encounters dangers first. On the other hand, she has access to food and water first and can chase away all inferior members of the group from any place at any time.

The stallion holds the herd together from a background position; he drives animals back to the herd and watches over his harem paying particular attention to possible rivals. One of the stallion's responsibilities is, obviously, reproduction. However, since the breeding season lasts for only a short period of the year, the common image of the macho stallion with only "one thing" on his mind is completely incorrect. Interactions between horses are determined by a strict pecking order. This hierarchy has a linear arrangement, compar-

Get off me: chasing away inferior group members does not always require a reason.

Four stallions, one gelding: not unusual but natural.

able to the rungs of a ladder, and each horse knows precisely who stands above whom. The pecking order is most obvious when the herd is on the move: established groups move slowly, one after the other, depending on the hierarchy.

You will have noticed that we talk about several mares but only one stallion. Where are the other stallions?

Although as many colts as fillies are born, every group of mares has only one stallion, but the others have to be somewhere! It is very simple: when the one to two year old youngsters are expelled from the herd, they form a bachelors' group.

Stallions build their own groups and they can sometimes be rough, but on no account do they fight each other for life and death.

In these social groups, young stallions grow and mature physically and mentally, and learn control as well as submission. Not every stallion can win a fight with an established herd stallion, winning his own mares as a reward. Life as a bachelor offers young and less successful, as well as older defeated stallions, a high quality of life in a stable community. To develop into socially competent horses that know how to behave confidently and with

Flight and play are reasons for faster speeds.

respect, stallions need to be allowed to mature within a herd, even when under the care of humans. Stallions that are kept in solitary confinement without social contacts and sufficient exercise inevitably turn into problem horses.

The spatial structure

We have already spoken about the "marching order" of the herd, with the dominant mare leading, followed by the other mares according to their rank, being driven and held together by the stallion.

They move slowly from A to B, usually at a leisurely walk as long as nothing causes the herd to flee.

On spacious pastures a herd will use the same paths, which after a while show as meandering tracks. These winding routes are chosen as they provide suitable observation of the area.

Our horses' need for exercise is inbred. Their ancestors had to cover wide areas to find enough food due to the low nutritional value of their main forage: grass of the plains. Researchers believe distances of up to 30 kilometres per day were common.

The main pace was the walk; only when running from danger or chasing each other – playfully or for real – did they go faster.

Comparing the living environment of a herd to a house, we see many "rooms", serving different purposes and with different equipment.

The dining room is the largest, equipped with sufficient grass of low nutritional value.

Resting places – bedrooms – are dry and exposed; they offer excellent visibility for watchful animals, allowing all herd members to sleep peacefully. It is not in the horse's nature to retire to an isolated resting place away from its companions.

The bathroom also serves as a barroom: not only can they satisfy their thirst but also a roll in the mud will get rid of troublesome insects – again a behaviour that is foreign to us humans! Naturally, such a bathroom à la horse is equipped with several rolling places, preferably provided with dry sand or a hard grass surface.

Personal space plays an important role in the spatial relationship between companions. Many species maintain a fixed distance between two individuals: for example, swallows lined up on a power line, keep regular spaces between them.

It is different for our horses: that

The rolling area stands out clearly from its surroundings.

Community of weanlings: personal space is suspended at resting times.

said, a certain space around every animal could be imagined and determined.

This space is different for every horse and situation, and can be infringed upon peacefully under certain conditions. Personal space therefore is not a fixed but a variable quantity.

Going back to the marching order, the distance between the highest ranking (leading mare) and lowest ranking (underling) horse is the greatest and horses of similar rank walk close together. However, very low ranking horses can sometimes be seen close to the leader while horses of similar rank are kept well at bay.

A possible explanation may be that competition between horses of a similar rank is naturally higher. A superior horse therefore has to watch its immediate companions more closely than a far lower ranking and therefore harmless underling.

Individual character, for example being good-natured or intolerant, may also play a role.

Generally, a low-ranking horse is

not permitted to intrude into the individual space of a superior horse. Social contacts, however, regularly reduce the distance between horses, for example during chasing games, mutual grooming and reproduction.

These and other activities are always initiated in the same way: encouragement to play, gently courting the mare or submission guarantee that reducing the individual distance cannot be misunderstood.

When grazing, individuals keep a relatively long distance from each other, which enables them to have a wide all-round view. If the herd stood closer together, only those on the outside would be able to see what was going on in the area. It is interesting that horses tend to stand parallel to each other, instead of facing different directions. This is most noticeable during grazing and resting in bad weather (wind and rain) and when sunbathing. When grazing, they slowly move in the same direction. In bad weather, the distance between the animals will be much smaller and the herd point their well-padded hindquarters towards the wind and rain. Sunbathing is done standing parallel to each other, exposing the flanks to the rays.

"Hey, are you playing with me?" Peaceful invasion of personal space.

The temporal structure

Horses live a relatively regulated life when left to their own devices: they tend to do the same thing at the same time, and often together. Even more important than the daily rhythm is something researchers call "time budget".

The time spent on certain activities is determined by the horse's gene pool, and if this conditioning cannot be fulfilled, stress will be generated; which will need to be released in other ways.

Horses living in the wild spend about 60 per cent of the day eating and walking slowly, about 20 per cent standing and a further 10 per cent lying down.

Other activities, such us grooming, take up the other 10 per cent of the day. The time frame is based on genetic predisposition.

Both factors produce what we can call "normal behaviour". Conditions that restrict horses' behaviour, or very different timetables, lead to stress and subsequently behavioural disorders and even health problems.

Solitary confinement in a box drastically reduces feeding times (due to feeding highly concentrated diets) and the need to exercise cannot be sufficiently satisfied. Behavioural researchers believe that this can cause many vices, which can be interpreted as displacing normal behaviour:

When the time budget for feeding is reduced, the resulting stress needs

Horses kept under such conditions cannot behave normally.

Horses will "dig out their food" only on snow-covered ground.

to be released in other ways. When twenty-three instead of a maximum of eight hours are spent resting, substitute exercise helps.

Only outdoor stable management in a group can guarantee a natural daily rhythm.

Horses' activities depend on many factors: some are unpredictable (for example, weather, supply of water and food, insects), some are periodical.

We therefore must be aware of seasonal as well as daily behavioural changes. When they are moulting, for example, horses spend more time grooming each other.

When the pasture is snow-covered, the snow has to be scraped away with the front legs; an activity obviously not found in the summer!

The following seasonal changes are important for the horse owner:

- In the autumn, the internal clock tells our horses to put on a layer of fat for the impending winter; a certain weight gain is therefore absolutely normal.
- The need to exercise seems less in the winter (reduction of energy consumption) and summer (heat, foals) than in spring and autumn.
- During breeding time, from early spring until summer, sexual behaviour is more apparent than during the other months.

On top of that, diurnal variations can be observed, although not as a strict timetable but more like alternating activities, for example:

- long spells of sunbathing immediately after sunrise,
- resting during the hottest hours of the day, and
- playing during the coolest hours.

There is a reason why herd members engage in the same activity at the same time: they all communicate with each other constantly, displaying what scientists call *mutual excitation*; mood is infectious within the group. Furthermore, being social animals, horses need to be with their companions. When the leading mare walks to the watering hole, the others will follow, even if not thirsty.

Communication in horse language

4

We have already discussed the hierarchy, mutual excitation within a herd and the regulating systems. These and other aspects of horses' social lives depend apon a unique form of communication. How else could sympathy and antipathy between horses be expressed and various moods be observed if not by transmission?

Communication amongst horses plays a critical role that is often underestimated by humans because it is much more subtle than ours.

When Paddy whinnies, everyone knows at once: a grown stallion calls.

Listen up!

Horses use sounds to communicate, just more quietly than we do. A call can be directed at companions but also at the whole herd or at people.

Contact is often established by neighing energetically across long distances; at close range a quiet grunt or bubbling noise is used as a greeting. During a fight, squealing (mares) or roaring (stallions) sounds are transmitted. Through these "personal" elements of language, information about the individual horse can be gathered, even to the human ear, especially about age and sex. Stallions whinny differently from mares, foals differently from adults.

Indirect expressions, however, like snorting when frightened or the groaning of an exhausted horse, are the same for every individual and have no personal characteristics.

One of the most important differences of the equine language in comparison to that of humans is the relatively small informative content: "Hello, is someone here?", "Go away, you irritate me!", "I'm after you!" or "Lovely to see you"; is probably all that is transmitted.

For the flight animal, it doesn't make much sense to talk loudly and to be heard by predators. They prefer other, more subtle ways of communication. They are true masters of this and so much better than people that we are no match for them.

Let the body talk

Horses use their whole body to communicate with their companions. It is possible for a horse to gather a lot of information about age, sex, rank and mood by a quick glance at their neighbour.

Indirect communication takes place as a type of background music. Specific body movements are aimed directly at the companion. This type of communication is called expressive behaviour. It describes all behavioural patterns used for communication.

I look into your eyes, Baby

Looking at a horse's face, people, even those inexperienced in body language, can tell a lot about the horse in question. Our horses have more or less distinctive sexual characteristics and situational faces.

Especially for the breeding animal, strong sexual characteristics are desired: one should be able to see from a distance whether it is a mare or a stallion, and this is usually not a problem.

Active breeding horses show strong sexual characteristics, while sports horses often have less distinctive features.

Brood mares look especially soft and motherly.

It is not easy to describe typical maternal or paternal faces with words. Pictures are a lot more revealing. Mares, in particular older brood mares, often have soft and, even by human standards, motherly faces, while stallions tend to look imperious and confident.

Depending on the situation, our horses show certain typical facial expressions.

If you threaten me I'll threaten you

When *dozing*, the lower lip drops down, the ears hang down either side or flop back and forth, the head and neck are lowered.

The grooming face can be observed well when stroking the animal. Usually horses groom each other (you groom me, I'll groom you) but if only one is groomed he or she will lengthen the neck, stretch out the upper lip and tilt the head.

A *frightened face* has the eyes wide open, the white of the eye is often visible, ears go back flat, and all facial muscles seem tense.

It is interesting that the *threatening face* looks quite similar. There can be a smooth transition between fearful (inferior) and confident (superior) threats.

A threatening horse often puts its ears back so flat that they disappear in the mane, but the panic-stricken expression is missing.

The ears of a frightened horse, however, are usually put back only slightly.

Nostrils and muzzle also indicate threat – the nostrils are narrowed, the corner of the muzzle is drawn back – or fear – the nostrils are widened, the muzzle is tense.

If the horse is interested in something, it shows an *exploring face*: its head is stretched forward in order to examine what is going on, the ears are pricked up, eyes wide open. If the horse is slightly unsure of the situation, it blows out air a couple of times.

Similarly, when horses see and greet each other, they show their exploring face and approach and touch each other gently with their noses.

After picking up each other's senses, intensive social contacts develop, like playing or grooming.

Concert of communication

The expression "concert of aids" is often used to describe the communication between rider and horse: a nice metaphor explaining the complexity and need for harmony.

Describing communication between species, the phrase "concert of expressions" can also be used,

During this chasing game, upright tails tell us: we are having fun!

It may look dangerous but the absence of threatening expressions shows us that these two stallions are only playing.

because every given message requires several movements or positions.

The above-mentioned faces are supported by certain movements of the whole body or of body parts. Of particular importance are:
- the tail;
- position of head and neck;
- the hindquarters and;
- body posture.

A few examples: the threatening face is used only on isolated occasions; this signal is often emphasized by a head toss towards the intruder (threatening posture), a threatening movement with the hindquarters or a head-on attack.

If a horse is interested in something, it will stare at the object of interest with its head and tail raised, the body tense and snorting heavily.

Should the inner tension become too great, it is released by running off: in case of real fear, with a frightened face, clamped tail, lowered position and at high speed; in case

The tail tells tales – tension instead of collection.

of a playful "flight", with raised tail, exploring face, high tension and in an elevated trot.

Watching fights between male horses, we can often observe them lashing out with their front legs. If it is a real fight it is accompanied by a threatening face; not so when only playing.

Certain behavioural patterns can only be interpreted correctly when observed in their entirety and the activity is not reduced to a single aspect.

Many behavioural patterns are of importance for the rider even when he or she wants to specifically deve-

lop or avoid them: an elevated trot (piaffe or passage) will only succeed when the natural confidence of a horse is not suppressed by fear of the rider.

Pricked up ears indicate that the horse's attention is certainly not directed at the rider. Ears put back flat indicate discomfort, fear or pain. Inner relaxation and easing of tension, so important for every aspect of good horse riding, are indicated by a quietly swinging tail – just watch horses at a high level dressage competition and you will notice that only a tenth of them are really relaxed!

5 Inherited or **learned?**

Breeders should pay attention to genetic aspects of behaviour.

When dealing with a behaviour that we consider difficult, the question is how do individual aspects of behaviour develop in the first place? We know that all horses have common behavioural patterns, as well as showing similar exterior characteristics distinguishing them from other species.

However, there must be individual qualities that we perceive as dysfunctional, or sometimes just as expressions of the horse's personality.

The horse lover will ask certain questions:

- How does a horse learn; how does it develop certain patterns of behaviour?
- How much of its behaviour is genetic, how much environmental?
- What are the causes for the development of vices, in the widest sense?
- What do I as a rider have to know about horse-specific patterns of learning?

Two views

Two fundamentally different opinions about the development of behaviour existed for a long time. One group of scientists believed that behaviour was inherited; the other group attributed every behaviour to environmental influences, and therefore thought it was acquired.

We have learnt only in recent years that both factors, hereditary and environmental, are responsible for the behaviour of an animal, and that these aspects cannot be separated from each other. Each behavioural feature is therefore the result of an interaction between genotype and environment. This relationship is expressed in the formula

ph=f(g,e)

where ph stands for phenotype (external feature), f describes a function, g stands for genetic and e for environmental aspect.

Breeders should know that not only characteristics like temperament and handling, but also a certain predisposition for the development of vices are genetic. Thoroughbreds (English and Arabian, or warmblood crosses) and offspring of certain stallions show these deviations sooner than others.

It is of particular importance for the horse owner to understand the relationship between environment and various behavioural patterns, and to recognise the limits of their own influence. In other words: what kind of environment do I have to offer my horse so that it can express its "normal" behaviour? Which mannerisms do I have to accept, whether I like them or not, because they are congenital and therefore cannot be changed?

Arabian thoroughbreds develop relatively more vices than other breeds.

Horses feel secure here; humans would rather retire to a cave.

All horses together

In order to secure the survival of the individual as well as the herd in the wild, our horses have adapted well to their environment throughout evolution.

As the horse's ancestors evolved, it proved beneficial to them:
- to organise a social group that improves the chances of survival even for its weakest member,
- being an unarmed herbivore, to develop into a flight animal that runs off first and then judges the situation,
- to be able to detect an exposed area that allows a good all-round view over the area, enabling them to flee in time,
- to be mobile, in order to walk long distances when food is scarce; and
- to regulate life in a community so that life-saving energy is not wasted on fights.

These fundamental characteristics and subsequent behaviour are inbred in all horses, and are resistant to human influence.

Maturing and learning processes

As mentioned before, experience has a great influence over the development of individual behaviour, in a positive as well as negative way. It is therefore of utmost importance to provide our horses with optimal surroundings from an early age onwards. Horses are quite flexible and are able to learn because they have had to adapt to changing environments again and again. Nevertheless, their adaptability has limits.

A problem can arise when there is no opportunity to learn, or a natural disposition is influenced by negative experiences in a way that complicates living with companions, endangers their own health and wellbeing and makes work with humans difficult.

The ethologist understands maturing as the perfection of innate behaviour without practice and therefore independent of experiences. The maturing process happens automatically, without environmental influence. Maturing processes are of less importance to the horse owner. More important is the real *learning process* of their horses, when dealing with specific behaviour and during training.

There are various ways of learning:
• Habit
• Classic conditioning
• Operational conditioning
• Imitation
• Insight
• Imprinting.

We must not forget that certain learning processes have a time limit: they take place within a well-

Two learning processes: learning through conditioning (mare follows person), and learning through imprinting (foal follows mare).

First time at the hairdresser's: this young Icelandic pony learns through habit that nothing bad is going to happen to him.

How horses learn

People with a very regular, predictable lifestyle are often called "creatures of habit". They seem unable to change or develop in any way. However; the word "habit" describes the exact opposite: when exposed to a stimulus again and again, and when this stimulus has neither positive nor negative associations for an animal, the importance of this stimulus will decrease with time – the animal has got used to it, it doesn't react to it any more.

This simple learning process can be used to change a horse's behaviour effectively, for example becoming accustomed to potentially threatening sights, noises or touches. Repeated exposure, when applied correctly, is useful for this learning process. We must remember, however, that the process is reversible.

The principle of *classic conditioning* cleverly connects two things that normally do not belong together. It is based on the fact that certain stimuli always cause a certain reaction (unconditional reflex), while other stimuli are of no consequence for the animal (neutral) and do not trigger a response. Classical conditioning could also be called an unconscious learning process, because the responses cannot be influenced by the mind.

Operational conditioning, also called "learning with an object", "trial and error", is different: conscious learning processes are taking place, consisting of an action and a reward. The animal carries out a

defined period, which is called the "sensitive phase". If a learning process is not completed during the sensitive phase, it cannot be completed in later life. The animal will have lost this process forever.

This is the case for imprinting, in particular.

Learning in stages: praise and treats encourage learning.

new movement and then experiences the fulfilment of a need that is seen as a reward (reinforcement).

After a few repeats a connection is made in the sense of "If I do this, then that will happen and I feel well". The new action has been learned. For the rider and horse owner, this is the principal way of learning during training. By rewarding and encouraging every step in the desired direction, the horse connects certain completed tasks with a positive feeling. The kind of reward can be different for every individual and can consist of a friendly word, a pleasant scratching of the mane, allowing the horse to stretch, or offering tasty treats.

The scientist also regards playing as a form of learning through success, defined as an actually pointless, positively "senseless" action. We see this "pretending" in the form of chasing, often in combination with fighting. Characteristic action games of horses involve wild gallops, bucking and jumping with impossible body contortions. Frequently these are started by one horse and then infect the whole herd.

Whether playful flight or mock fights between stallions, the intention to play is indicated shown using certain signals that prevent misunderstandings and stop the whole herd from running off in a wild panic, just because a youngster

Playful behaviour is usually expressed more often by young horses, and more by male than female animals.

Boisterous encounters, with all the elements of a stallions' fight, only accidentally lead to minor injuries; as long as all parties are socially competent.

Imitation can also be called learning through observation. The horse benefits from the experience of others; it copies this behaviour. Foals in particular learn through imitation; for example, by watching their mothers graze, they learn to distinguish tasty from unpalatable grass. Slightly older or adult horses are also able to modify their own behaviour through imitation.

When riding a young horse, the company of an experienced, older horse can be of enormous benefit when trying new tack or dealing with "dangerous" situations. This real learning process must not be confused with the transmission of moods when the same behaviourisms are shown at the same time through imitation. These mannerisms, however, do not need to be learned again; they are already part of the individual's behavioural range.

Learning through insight, also called *cognitive behaviour*, is a particularly high achievement of the mind. This form of learning requires that an animal is able to predict the consequences of an event even before it has started, and that it can act appropriately. The current scientific opinion is that horses are not able to do this, unlike humans and primates.

The foal learns through imitation to distinguish palatable grass from others.

has a mad moment: instead of a threatening or frightened face, friendly expressions, relaxed postures and often raised tails signal the players' good intentions.

Even though it may be boring, the follow action has to be learnt.

Mental processes, like feigning lameness to avoid competing at the weekend, are far beyond the abilities of even the most cunning horse.

Through imprinting, even a newborn foal will learn to recognise its mother (bonding reaction). This process starts immediately after birth and is completed at about two days of age, and cannot be changed afterwards.

It is not without reason that the mare protects her foal vehemently during this phase and also keeps a very close contact - physically, and by smell and voice. Disturbances during this time can lead to erroneous bonding and the foal may then connect closely with a foster parent, for example humans.

As this has negative effects on the horse's whole development, including sexual imprinting and social behaviour, people should not interfere too much during this time.

Imprint training, where the foal is subjected to various manipulations by humans, is very dangerous and also of doubtful ethical value.

6

Typical horse!
Functions of equine behaviour

Every movement can be defined as behaviour – a horse cannot **not** behave. We should avoid concentrating only on difficult behaviour, on behaviour in relation to contact with humans; or on behaviour solely relevant to our requirements. The interaction of all aspects of its inate and learned behaviour represents what we recognise as "typical horse".

Always on the move – movement behaviour

We know that horses are herd and flight animals. The definition of "flight" and "running" suggests movement at higher speeds, but that is not always so. In reality, horses like it slow; their main and preferred pace is the walk.

Wild horses would spend the main part of the day grazing. Living on the plains, they were used to walking slowly ("pasture walk"), one leg after the other, across poor pastures. That way, they could cover significant distances per day and were on the move for up to 15 - 16 hours. They walked between the watering holes, resting and rolling places at a leisurely pace, in single file.

Reasons for higher speeds were and still are particularly flight, games and fights.

When a horse becomes aware of a threatening stimulus it will immediately flee at high speed. Depending on how strong the stimulus is and whether it is persistent or not, the horse will stop its flight at a fast gallop and then fall into a trot, usually with a very tense body. The fleeing horse will eventually stop and look around with its head up high and tense. Air is often expelled loudly. The tension will be released by a few jumps. Only after having analysed the situation thoroughly, will the horse calm down and return to its original activity.

Horses deal with dangerous situations very differently from humans, and this repeatedly leads to problems.

Two aspects in particular are relevant for the assessment of the situation: first, the horse's propensity to flee from stimuli that humans consider perfectly harmless; secondly, the "contagiousness" within a social group. If one horse is frightened, all of them become scared. Horses rely

Shared walks reinforce the bond between humans and horses, because they appeal to the horse's nature.

on each other, and they have become herd animals not least because it gives them a better opportunity to watch their surroundings.

When playing, horses show different aspects of movement behaviour in a "senseless" context. These movements are often exaggerated and can be understood, in connection with gestures and body language, as pretence. Favourites are movement games, ranging from chasing, fighting to running independently from each other, but carried out at the same time. Horses may play on their own (solitary games) but more often together (social games), and they encourage each other by nudging, pinching the other one gently or circling their potential partner.

Sometimes, a horse starts a solitary game and encourages the others. Chases are interrupted by fights, that then develop into a wild chase once more.

Tension is often released by performing the craziest manoeuvres: bucking, kicking and lashing out with the front legs, often accompanied by wild squeals.

Fighting games have set rules.

During serious fights, especially between stallions in the breeding season, we can detect many elements that will be familiar from advanced dressage. Piaffe, passage, lateral movements, levade and pesade are not unnatural, forced movements but normal elements of motion. Admittedly, in the wild we find these original movements mostly in stallions, while mares display less distinctive manoeuvres. Ranking fights amongst mares are executed mainly by the parties standing hind-quarter to hindquarter, kicking and trying to push each other away, accompanied by indignant squeals.

A stallion driving his mares has a very typical position: his ears flat back and head lowered, he carries out sideways movements with his head and neck while chasing single mares back to the herd or driving the whole group on.

If one of the ladies does not react, biting and pinching can follow, usually to the rump or hocks. Simple movements, like threatening with a

Age is no protection from games, but this is too much for Monty (30 years old), who signals a warning with his hind leg.

head toss or the hindquarters, have already been mentioned.

On the subject of movement: horses in the wild only jump if there is no alternative. No horse will jump voluntarily ...

It is clear that horses' general motion behaviour cannot be separated from their other functional behaviours: feeding and social behaviour including playing and fighting are closely connected to certain movements.

Excretion and social behaviour

It may seem somewhat peculiar to consider the excretion of urine and faeces in the context of social behaviour, but indeed it is a vital element of behaviour. This is an important consideration for the horse owner, who will have to allow for some aspects when designing the living environment.

Even looking at the silhouette, urinating mares…

… can be distinguished from geldings and stallions.

Dollar examines the droppings of his competition.

Horses urinate, depending on water intake and loss through sweat, every four to five hours, and often immediately after work or longer resting periods.

Horses always remain standing when urinating. They extend their front legs forward, spread the hind legs wide and angle them slightly – it makes space so that no urine can splash on legs or belly. This is also the reason why many horses are reluctant to perform on hard surfaces. They prefer to wait until they find soft ground.

As we know only too well, no outstanding performance can be achieved with a full bladder. A tense back and reluctance to move are often a sign of the urge to urinate. The rider should then halt, let the reins go and either stand or sit light to allow the horse to urinate without hindrance. Normally, the horse will then relieve itself, often with a sigh, but some special ones insist on being dismounted, and even having the saddle taken off – otherwise they cannot perform! Longer hacks therefore have to be planned to allow sufficient rest. During a break, horses should be tied up in a way that enables them to relieve themselves.

Droppings can be produced on the move, although it is the exception and must be enforced by the rider. Even if a sensitive rider finds this hard, he or she should always insist on it, otherwise the horse may suddenly stop while crossing a busy road, to answer nature's call.

As non-territorial animals, the ancestors of our horses used defecation to transmit messages. Conse-

Grazing should take place only in areas that are free of droppings, but what do they do in a stable?

to other herd members! Stallions especially explore the droppings thoroughly, scrape them apart, and then cover them with their own faeces or urine and check again.

Any horse covering the droppings of his boss is in trouble – this is immediately interpreted as provocation, and punished! Defecation is also used to underline one's own rank.

Despite this interest in excrement, droppings and urine are generally avoided when grazing or selecting resting places. Wild horses would rarely come into close contact with droppings, and therefore appropriate actions (like burying them) were not necessary. Conspicuous places were used to excrete, presumably due to their signalling effect.

Domesticated horses tend to favour certain places on a pasture, too, often along fences, in corners, on top of molehills or similar areas, for their droppings.

Unfortunately, it is impossible for stabled horses to avoid their own excrement. They are forced to rest on a surface of urine and faeces, and eat their hay on it. This is not only unhygienic because of endoparasite contamination, but also because of damage to their lungs and the often reduced resting times. Decaying excrement releases aggressive substances, especially ammonia, that are then inhaled when lying down, attacking the sensitive mucous membranes in the airways.

Many stallions show similar behaviour in a stable as outside. Droppings are left in one corner and the rest of the box is kept immaculately clean.

quently, excretion plays an important role in their social behaviour: the way of defecation, the droppings themselves and the pheromones in them transmit information, particularly about sex and rank. This is why droppings are of some interest

Rest well – resting behaviour

Whilst talking about lying down: the resting behaviour of horses is very different from our own needs. As flight animals, the wild ancestors of our horses could not afford to sleep deeply for several hours each night. They would not have survived for long.

They developed sophisticated mechanisms that enabled them to find the necessary rest, despite constant threats. They have kept these techniques to this day. Characteristic are:

- splitting resting times into many short intervals,
- developing various forms of resting,
- preferring open, dry and warm places, and
- being close to watchful other horses, especially when deeply asleep.

Horses spend about 30 per cent of the day resting; two to three hours lying down and a further five hours standing, in intervals of around 20 minutes. Foals rest for significantly longer and lie down more, while very old horses hardly lie down at all because getting up is too much effort. Resting periods are more frequent during the night, but also occur during the day when it is very hot (summer) or immediately after sunrise (sunbathing).

These times are kept under natural conditions and with proper management. However, the stabled horse must rest – necessarily – for 80 to 90 per cent of the day!

Swishing tails chase away tormenting insects.

Horses usually stand and doze in pairs or groups. They are positioned one behind the other or head to tail in order to keep the flies away from their faces. In the warm season the body is exposed to the sun; during bad weather the hindquarters are held towards the wind. Horses standing and resting have a dozing face and relaxed body, with the neck positioned almost horizontally.

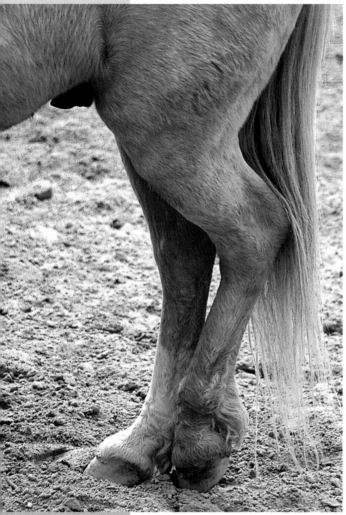

The resting hind leg can relax; the other one carries the body weight without muscle strength

A special anatomical system (passive stay apparatus) enables the horse to take the load off its hindquarters. The kneecap can be fixated over a bony ridge and the limb is locked without using its muscular strength. One leg can carry the hindquarters without having to use energy. The other one is relieved, and the hoof is usually positioned on its toe.

Horses awake out of this dozing within split seconds and are ready to flee. Horses lie down for a deeper rest, preferably on a dry and warm sur-face with a good grip. They bend their front legs and roll their shoulder into a **sternal position**. The hind legs are pulled towards the abdomen, the front legs kept bent and half underneath the chest. Many horses prefer to lie on one side, which can be seen by the distribution of dirt on their body. The head is either held free with a typical dozing face or, when resting more deeply, the eyes are closed and the muzzle propped on the ground. In this sternal position, horses doze or lightly sleep.

For deep sleep, horses go into a **lateral position** by stretching out their front legs and lying down with head and neck on the ground. In this position they show all the signs of deep sleep known as REM, a particularly intense and mentally relaxing form of rest. The expression stems from the involuntary movements of the eyes (rapid eye movements) during this phase. Anyone who takes the time to observe horses without disturbing them will be surprised to notice that they do obviously dream. They show movements of their legs, ear and eyes, sometimes whinny or bubble, as though they were in an intense dream. Foals rest in a lateral position for significantly longer than adults, but adults too, need a restful sleep lying down to assure their physical and mental well-being.

Horses get up by pulling their hind legs underneath their body

Deep sleep in a lateral position is only possible when the horse feels secure.

and stretching their front legs straight out.

Then head and neck are swung forward, hind legs straightened and the horse can get up.

As a flight animal, the horse needs security to be able to rest and relax. The presence of watchful other horses provides this, especially when lying down and not being able to run off quite so quickly. Members of a herd never all lie down at the same time. There is always one keeping an eye on the area to warn the sleeping colleagues of any threat. In conventional boxes, visual contact is disrupted when lying down, which has negative consequences for length and quality of these important resting times. Species-specific stable management has to bear in mind the sleeping habits of horses. A clean, dry and soft surface in an open yet protected position should

Eating and drinking – feeding behaviour

Protected by an adult, the weanlings can doze safely.

In connection with movement behaviour, we mentioned that grazing horses spend many hours per day moving slowly forward. Throughout evolution, horses living on the plains have adapted to continuously eating small amounts of poor feed. Domesticated horses have the same basic eating requirements as their ancestors, which have to be taken into consideration to avoid physical as well as psychological problems. Not only "what" but also "how" they eat is important.

Under natural conditions, herd members often graze together and spend about half the day eating, either having small snacks or a substantial main meal, the latter usually in the morning and evening.

Their biorhythm demands continuous activity and their digestive system is designed to cope with small amounts of low concentrated feed.

Large portions of hard feed and limited forage, or infrequent, large meals therefore lead not only to physical but also psychological disturbances. The less a domesticated horse has to do, the more important is the time spent eating, even if it is spent in one place and not moving around – eating while standing still is better than boredom!

Horses have a favourite eating position: walking across a pasture, one leg is put in front of the other one so that the head can be comfortably lowered to the ground. Eating in this relaxed position is

be reserved as a resting place, and not be used for other purposes.

Too much activity (for example in proximity to a water trough) causes disturbance and prevents lower ranking horses, in particular, from resting adequately.

Wrongly designed open stables with muddy ground and no separation of functional areas stops horses from lying down.

The food is examined carefully with the lips.

only possible if the food is at ground level; head-high hayracks are therefore not recommended. Troughs can be positioned at chest height, since hard feed is eaten in a short period of time.

The sensitive lips help to select preferred grass and form a tuft, which is then seized with the front teeth and ripped out by moving the head sideways. The food is ground with the molars and then swallowed.

Eating hard feed, horses also show intensive lip movements and they can even manage to single out the odd unpalatable grain or pellet from the feed.

Grass, herbs and legumes form the main part of the wild horse's diet, together with smaller amounts of reed, tree bark and other plants.

Horses also like whole branches of poplars, willows or fruit trees, that will be carefully peeled and sometimes even completely chewed and eaten – something to do for bored horses!

Two aspects of eating behaviour often lead to problems: horses prefer sweet-tasting food and they do not feel full like we do. If we eat too much, a signal will be sent to the brain by stretch sensors in our stomach wall and we stop eating.

Horses do not have receptors like that. They seem to feel full only after enough chewing movements, sufficient time spent feeding or fatigue of the chewing muscles.

Reed, leaves and bark are part of the natural diet of our horses.

The tendency of well-meaning horse owners to offer their four-legged friends plenty of hard feed and not enough hay and straw upsets their horse's digestive system. Naturally, horses prefer the hard feed that is often enhanced by molasses or similarly palatable substances, but because it does not need to be chewed hard, it does not satisfy the stomach.

Although sufficient nutrients have been ingested, the horse still feels hungry. It will either demand, and get, seconds and soon suffer from digestive problems, or it will look for an alternative occupation and develop a behavioural problem.

Even when properly kept, the innate eating requirements of horses have to be satisfied.

If there is not enough space at the feeding area, lower-ranking horses will be constantly disturbed and may not even be allowed sufficient access to food. Several solutions can prevent this:

- In small groups, several food troughs are placed in different parts of the shelter, plus one more than necessary. If a horse is chased away it can still find a filled trough. This solution may be a bit complicated and costly, but is certainly effective.

- With enough space, a long feed bar is installed that assures sufficient distance between horses.

- If space is limited and horses are to be fed individually, feed stands are recommended. These stands should be closed at the sides, with only small gaps, be deep and narrow (the measurements vary according to the size of the horse) in order to allow lower-ranking horses to eat without disruption. Some stands can be closed from behind.

- Computerised feeders that allow an individual amount of food to be offered are expensive. In combination with an intricate system of pathways, they allow the feeding of small amounts, encouraging walking activities. The only disadvantage is that horses must eat alone and not like nature intended, in groups. This can lead to jealousy.

When drinking, species-specific behaviour can be observed too. How often and how much a horse drinks in a day depends on the surrounding temperature, exercise and the water content in the food, but amounts of 10 litres per 100kg body weight are absolutely normal. Horses interrupt the drinking process, similarly to eating, several times to observe their surroundings. If everything is all right, they lower their head to the water surface, close their lips almost completely and suck the water through the small remaining gap.

There are different and contradictory opinions about the preferred water quality.

There are various reports about competition horses – mainly of high blood types – that will not drink in unfamiliar surroundings. When competing or racing somewhere else, not only food but also water from home has to be provided. Horses living in the wild cannot afford to be that fussy; therefore we suspect a mistake that occurred

The horse can eat from a low trough in a natural way.

There is fresh water at the stables, but Topper prefers this muddy puddle – who knows why?

during rearing. A foal learns from its mother and through imitation which food is suitable. As this is the case for water as well, we guess that a limited choice of water sources prevents a horse from accepting other qualities.

It is said that horses do not drink water contaminated with dirt, algae or faeces, but there are opposing reports of horses that actually prefer such water. Whether this is also caused by a mistake during rearing, or whether there are good reasons for it is not known.

When installing a water source, several aspects of social and eating behaviour should be considered. Watering areas in immediate proximity to favourite resting places are often almost blockaded by high-ranking animals and may not be accessible to others for long periods. In large herds or amongst unfriendly members, the installation of several water places is recommended. Water sources next to hayracks are often misused for soaking hay, which is not ideal for digestion. It is better to keep sufficient distance and so make life a little harder for our lazy friends.

Queuing up for drinking: one drinking-trough is not enough.

Even in a crowd, family bonds and ranking orders rule.

In good company – social behaviour

Certain aspects of social behaviour have been mentioned in previous chapters. It should have become clear that it is impossible for a horse to develop any natural behaviour without companions, and that all other functions are strongly influenced by the presence or absence of other horses.

A *horse alone is not a horse* – meaning, horse-specific behaviour is only possible in a group; when kept alone, strong deviations from, and disturbances of normal behaviour will develop.

If all of these deviations from a norm were a disadvantage for humans, species-specific stable management would have infiltrated traditional areas of sport and breeding. However, many disturbances are not easily recognised, or they have already become an accepted and therefore "normal" part of horse keeping.

Just walk with open eyes and ears through a stable that has not been designed properly and count the number of horses exhibiting signs of disturbance – crib biting, weaving, and aggression against other horses or humans, uncontrollability under the saddle – and then do the same test in a natural stable: you will become a converted campaigner for a species-specific stable management!

Although the combination of social behaviour and functional groups has already been discussed, the basics of living together will be repeated. The social structure of a herd is determined by family relations and ranking order. The organisation of the herd guarantees safety, independent of a horse's rank – safety not only from the potential dangers outside, but also from within the group. The ranking order allocates everyone their place and regulates all aspects of communal living, without first having to establish these. Who avoids whom, who has the priority of getting to water and food, who will get the best resting place, who is in the lead and who is being led; these and more are the automatic result of the rank of the individual and the companions with whom they are in social contact.

A high rank is not given but must be earned. Qualities that render the individual valuable for the herd, so-called "leadership qualities", are important. Physical superiority, amongst other things, is crucial, but experience and authority are also essential. High-ranking horses do not stand out because of their aggression against other herd members: they usually solve problems through small gestures and expressive mimes – that is enough.

You can't practise too much, if you want to become a stallion.

Stallions on their own: it looks wild but has an order.

Age, fighting experience and maturity make a leader, and it is often a horse which we do not recognise as one.

Despite their tendency to settle fights amicably, conflicts in natural herds as well as in groups selected by people do happen, although serious injuries are very rare. Most rows are solved peacefully by using threatening gestures to put the opponent in his place, and rivals submit to this by avoiding actions, fleeing, or appropriate gestures of (empty chewing, turning away). Physical fights show sex-specific patterns and follow strict rules that prevent most injuries. This form of

ritualised fighting is also called competition fighting.

Stallions and geldings rear in front of each other, kneel down and bite their fore legs. They circle each other, bite into their hindquarters. They carry out these and other movements almost simultaneously, although they could attain an advantage by breaking the rules. In order to end a clash or serious fight without severe injuries, the defeated horse must have the opportunity to flee. It is rare that the situation escalates; in the wild, such fights only happen amongst stallions in the presence of mares, when they can have a lethal outcome.

As mentioned before, young stallions live peacefully with each other, and even mature stallions are not usually bloodthirsty tyrants, but caring fathers.

Fighting games follow similar patterns, but threatening gestures are missing and there is no final decision when one opponent gives up. On the contrary, there could be alternating roles of "winner" and „loser", and both playing partners may nibble each other's faces gently.

Under human care, the same rules apply, although a thoughtless change of herd members and numerous other variations increase the likelihood of conflicts. Mistakes when designing a stable or pasture (lack of space, dead corners) can lead to more frequent injuries. Socially incompetent horses are a constant source of trouble because they are not familiar with the rules of everyday life and are not experienced with species-specific communication. Open stable groups live peacefully when:

• their groups remain the same over a long period of time,
• mares and geldings are kept separately (stallions and geldings can often be kept together),
• members of one group are of similar age and size (exception: weanlings and "aunts" or "uncles"),
• the area is well structured by separating functional places and integrating dividing elements in order to provide retreats and it allows every horse to access such a functional place at any time without disturbance.

Please scratch here – comfort behaviour

Body care is important for horses, even if their priorities are different from ours. It is not surprising that mutual grooming – social body care – is of greater value than nursing one's body alone.

When approaching, the initiator shows a "grooming face" with a friendly expression and typically extended upper lip. Even foals practise grooming with great devotion and at length. Characteristic is a reversed parallel position in which both horses nibble the same body parts with their teeth. They concentrate particularly on areas they cannot reach themselves, i.e. crest, withers and the back down to the rump.

Horses are very inventive when grooming. They gnaw with their incisor teeth and reach front legs, chest, flanks and hind legs. The hind foot can be used to scratch the head. Careful: if the horse wears a head collar it can get trapped in it and will then fall, and can even die of subsequent shock.

Sharp objects are used with great care to scratch the face or ears, and also the back or rump and belly. If the eyes are itchy due to an untreated condition, a horse can rub them so violently on its front legs that it can result in cornea injuries. Tree trunks are mainly used to rub the mane and tail.

If this becomes excessive and a horse is seen to engage in social or solitary grooming too intensively, it

Male friendship: Chris rubs and Dollar enjoys.

Social grooming strengthens the bond between friends.

can be a sign of certain diseases (sweet itch, pinworm or lice).

Rolling is very important for the horse; an all-round treatment for the coat that is of particular importance for their well-being. Horses kept under human care prefer rolling after being worked, especially when sweaty. If a stabled horse does not have enough room for a satisfying roll, it can often get trapped in a position, making it impossible to get up by itself. When lacking the opportunity to roll, the horse should be let loose in the schooling arena or in a fenced-in area with soft ground in order to allow it to carry out this essential activity.

The horse will lie down in a sternal position first, but then stretches out on its side and rub its head and neck thoroughly. It will have several attempts at including the back and rump as well.

With a bit of practice it will manage to roll over onto the other side, where the procedure is repeated. After getting up, it will shake itself with its legs spread apart, and the shaking movement will continue through the body like a wave from the front to the back. It will often blow out air fiercely because of inhaled dust.

Horses prefer uncovered, dry, sandy or hard places. When tormented by insects, however, they choose a damp rolling place to acquire a mud crust that offers very effective protection. Horses are very fussy when choosing a suitable location and they search with a lowered nose for an ideal spot, which is then further explored by scraping with their front legs.

A frequent going down and getting up without rolling, or only short spells on one side, often

Dry places are preferred for rolling.

Sand and dust, but also old hair, dirt and sweat fly off.

accompanied by beating the hind legs against the belly or looking round at the flank, is a typical symptom of colic.

Horses that are close to each other strengthen their bond by mutual grooming. Grooming carried out by people has a similar effect. The horse lover should not only perform the usual cleaning before work, but a heartfelt stroke along the mane can also be used as praise and confirmation of a friendly relationship, in a manner comprehensible to the horse. A loud clapping on the side

of the neck, however, will probably just confuse the horse.

While horses kept in boxes on their own can only perform solitary grooming, and even that is often difficult (getting trapped when rolling), open stable management offers plenty of opportunities for solitary and social body care. This can be controlled by certain measures. Rolling places laid out with sand, sawdust, straw or tree bark, fenced-in and with a roof effective rement. Smooth, bark-free tree trunks or special rubbing devices with brushes (these are made for cattle, and are available in agricultural merchants) are particularly good for horses suffering from sweet itch, and will prevent them from rubbing off their manes on rough surfaces or even injuring themselves.

Sexual behaviour

Sad but true: many committed horse owners never have the opportunity to observe a horse's family life at first hand. Artificial ways of reproduction are already normality, despite all the disadvantages.

Just one problem amongst many: not all deviations from normality are the result of experiences and environmental factors, but it has been discovered that a predisposition for certain behavioural disturbances can be inherited. If such a disturbance affects reproduction, the horse in question would not normally be able to produce any offspring, and the problem would solve itself.

The reality is, however, that the behaviour of the participating horses is of no importance for breeding any more; humans have replaced nature with technique.

Foals mimic sexual behaviour from in early age – even Mummy is used.

Although Tonka is in season, she still pushes him away.

If normal behaviour is no longer a selection criterion, horses that are chosen for reproduction can carry severe inherited vices without it being noticed. Assuming this continues for many generations, one can end up with a stallion that would be infertile under natural circumstances, and an unproductive mare.

But how do our horses reproduce under natural conditions – like hedgehogs, very very carefully? One could say so because, although courtship and mating contain some aggressive elements, it is generally a gentle and ritualised affair. Under natural circumstances, young horses have plenty of time and space to gain experience: they watch the herd stallion, experience the behaviour of their mothers or of their many "aunts" and they themselves show elements of sexual behaviour, such as mounting when still only foals.

At an age of roughly one a half years, fillies and colts are theoretically fertile. Under natural conditions, however, they will not yet reproduce, as the young stallions are only able to win mares with increasing physical and mental maturity and young mares will not become pregnant when mated too early.

This means that the growing mares conceive only when they are physically prepared.

Not only the stage of development, but also many other factors, determine reproductive success. Horses, in particular mares, are seasonal breeders and cyclic.

Increasing daylight in January will start hormonal activity. In the period up to summer, the mares will be in season every three weeks for about five days. The "heat" can be divided into pre-oestrus, oestrus and post-oestrus.

The mare will stand only during oestrus; at other times she will kick the stallion away.

The stallion on the other hand checks and smells the mare's excretions and is able to recognise the phase of the cycle from the excreted pheromones. The mare will then indicate whether she is in season or not.

During oestrus the mare signals her readiness by lifting and turning her tail, flashing (rhythmic movements of the vulva), and standing with her hind legs apart. Finally, she will accept being mounted. Mares in season try to attract attention from geldings as well, and these often attempt – unsuccessfully, of course – to mate them.

Mares in season also change their behaviour towards people significantly, especially when being ridden. They often become very lazy, and react to the pressure from the rider's leg not with more but less speed – the mare "confuses" the leg aids with the clinging legs of the stallion, and would rather stop.

Stallions also show some seasonality, although it is determined by the presence of mares in oestrus. During the breeding season stallions are more easily distracted, and are less co-operative and more aggressive towards other stallions. They do not think exclusively, but more intensely, about the "one thing". Nevertheless, the common picture of the macho stallion who is always ready is absolutely wrong. Stallions are very careful when approaching a mare, not least because they could be kicked and possibly injured by a mare that is not yet ready to be mated. A daredevil that just jumps on a mare will feel the lady's hind legs where it hurts most, while a willing and prepared mare does not show any aggression.

Under natural conditions the stallion always stays directly or indirectly in contact with his mares: driving them, grooming or checking their scents. A long time before the actual mating takes place, he will start to court his chosen one by approaching her again and again, seeking contact, exploring her scent intensely or licking her, but he will always keep a respectful distance from her hind legs. Until the mare is ready, she will not tolerate any attempt at being mounted, and will avoid the stallion, or actively fend him off.

The stallion will wait for the right moment when the behaviour of the mare changes, but he can also stimulate her by gentle foreplay.

After the foreplay the stallion mounts the standing mare and, after a few attempts, inserts his erect

Stallions stay in continuous contact with their companions by checking their droppings.

penis. He leans on the rump of the mare, embraces her with his front legs and props his mouth up on her withers. Some stallions also bite into the crest to stabilise themselves. After a few thrusting movements the stallion ejaculates and slides off the mare, who he will mate a few times more during her oestrus.

If the mare conceives, she will give birth after around eleven months, foaling usually in the early morning hours.

The end of the pregnancy is announced by typical signs, parti-cularly the development of an udder and sinking of the abdomen.

Disturbances during the opening phase can delay the birth, as the mare needs to feel safe.

Immediately after birth the mare actively initiates contact by tou-ching and licking her foal and a bond is established, particularly through the foal's smell, but also its appearance and voice.

Foals are born as flight animals and are therefore incredibly capable straight after birth. It takes less than an hour until the foal can stand and

During the first few days after birth the mare will be in permanent contact with her offspring.

starts looking for the udder, supported by the mother who positions herself in a suitable reverse parallel way.

First learning successes happen quickly, which makes the important movements easier for the foal. Newborn foals are soon able to follow their mothers, and although the follow reaction is inherited, the mare has to teach her foal first (imprinting). The foal has to learn who its mother is, which can take up to two days. Therefore the mare often does not tolerate any contact by other horses or people, because it can lead to false imprinting.

While suckling, the bond with the mother remains, but the foal will build relationships with other youngsters, with whom it will spend more and more time. The new friendships, reinforced by social grooming and games, also

A lot of exercise for the foal and nourishing food for mummy: a good start to life.

help the foal through weaning, which under natural circumstances never occurs before eight months of age. Early weaning, at not much more than four months, as practised by many breeders, can traumatise the physically and mentally immature foal, and can lead to behavioural problems later on in life. Other mistakes in the upbringing, especially keeping mare and foal in a stable, keeping a youngster without companions of the same age, or starting work too early, can be disastrous and lead to problems that are more or less incurable. Properly brought up horses, however, are easier to educate, are full of the joys of life, and perform well up to an old age and are therefore a delight for their riders.

7

Hot topic:
the problem horse

Something is wrong here: how to "create" a problem horse

Although latest research suggests that a certain genetic predisposition is involved, generally speaking problem horses are made and not born. Behavioural disturbances are always the result of too much pressure: we must not forget that despite their great flexibility, domesticated horses cannot overcome inherited limitations.

True behavioural disturbances are the result of the horse being forced in a situation that is beyond its adaptability. Such circumstances create tension, because normal behavioural patterns can no longer be expressed (deprivation). The trigger for these patterns still exists, but the expression is blocked (frustration) or two equally strong behaviourisms are activated and consequently inhibit each other (conflict).

This tension will finally be released by a deviation from normal behaviour and this is, strictly speaking, a perfectly "normal" reaction. One could say that behavioural disturbances are natural reactions of horses to an unnatural environment. They offer an outlet for stress that cannot be released in any other way; this must not be forgotten.

Every horse has natural mechanisms to release stress, because wild or naturally kept horses also experience deprivation, frustration and conflict. A known reaction is substitution, also called a displacement activity. If a horse faces a conflict when two needs are equally strong and inhibit each other, the solution can be to carry out a third, not exactly related activity. As soon as this and other adaptation techniques no longer work, behavioural disturbances occur.

Difficult behaviour can build up when certain factors come together: improper keeping, incorrect handling and mistakes during training can be single, but also collective causes. Behind these, however, are always horse owners and riders who may mean well but who are not sufficiently informed.

Under which circumstances can vices develop, when looking at it from a human point of view?

Problems occur when we transfer our own requirements to our horses. A horse lover who is unfamiliar with

Every contact with horses, even the most gentle, is strictly speaking a form of manipulation.

normal horse behaviour will find the inevitable fights in a herd stressful, worries about lack of shelter and does not want to expose his horse to the elements.

For horses as with humans, social life does not always run smoothly: at times experience there are major setbacks, but we learn and grow with the highs and lows. The unfa-

Being turned out should not be a privilege of robust pony breeds: warmbloods too want to get out of their boxes!

miliar owner overlooks the fact that horses have to feel a part of the herd in order to gain inner security. They – unlike us – will not regard an isolated box as a safe haven. Frost, rain and wind do not worry our horses as much as they do their freezing, hairless owners, and there is always enough room in a good open stable with a roof. Even the lowest ranking horse (normal behaviour provided) is at all times a respected and protected member of the herd.

No horse will flee into a stable when facing danger. And no horse will become ill just because it is wet and dirty.

Problems will certainly occur when the uninformed horse owner regards the differences in breeds as the reason for various forms of stable management. What is right for wild ponies surely has to be wrong for elegant sports horses? A false conclusion. First, even the most highly bred horse has the same basic requirements as the most robust pony. Secondly, competition horses can be kept in a herd in an open stable too, without adverse consequences for health and performance or workload and finances. This can be seen in exemplary yards where, for example, high class dressage horses are kept in groups of four to six in open stables.

If natural stable management was in place everywhere, chronic airway diseases, premature wear and tear and many vices would soon be the exception rather than the rule.

Problems will inevitably occur when horses and humans cannot communicate with each other. Horses kept on their own are literally anti-social because their communication skills are only partially developed. Communication has to be learned, practised and constantly refined. These socially inept horses often show erratic behaviour, causing the owner to learn more about corrective methods at weekend courses or from books. Two traps await the unsuspecting horse lover: the mistaken belief that a few, quickly acquired exercises and techniques can correct any problem horse, and that behavioural disturbances can be improved by dominant training. Prevention is better than any cure, a knowledgeable owner better than any expert, and good horsemanship better than any new technique.

Problems can occur when, while searching for the reasons for abnormal behaviour, cause and effect become confused. If a horse starts weaving only when there is riding activity in its immediate vicinity, it would be wrong to try and solve the problem by keeping the horse in a box in an isolated part of the yard. It is not the riding activity, but the non-stimulating isolation in the box that is the real cause. An everyday event like riding can be the trigger for erratic behaviour when the horse is constantly lacking a stimulus. Equally wrong are "corrective therapies" that merely suppress the

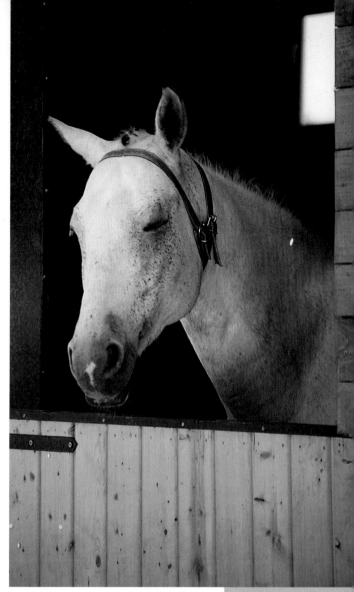

Crib-biting belts: do they really help the horse?

symptoms of the vice (special gates to prevent weaving, belts for crib-biters). They often only worsen the horse's stress and cause further problems.

Feeding calming herbs or installing toys in the box, or a double bridle for strong horses, are methods that are adressing the symptoms, rather than the cause, of undesirable behaviour.

Problems also develop when people forget that horses learn both unwelcome and desired types of behaviour equally quickly, or when they do not pay full attention to what they are actually teaching their horses.

A practical example: a young and impatient pony must learn to stand still when tied up. It is then tied up and the owner goes away. Left alone and without understanding the aim of the exercise, the youngster will show its impatience by pawing the ground forcefully. The juvenile owner immediately returns, hits the pony with the stick and shouts at it. What does the pony learn?

When it paws the ground it will be paid attention and is not alone any more; when the owner comes back it will hurt....Is that a good learning success? People may be more intelligent than horses, but what they do with it is sometimes a different matter!

A checklist of problem behaviour

It is not the purpose of this book to illustrate the whole range of erratic patterns, be it abnormal or undesired behaviour.

It has certainly become clear that by informed design of the living environment, many problems can be avoided and that the horse lover should pay closest attention to

Impatient pawing is not a reason for punishment.

These two prove that proper management of stallions is possible for warmbloods as well as for Icelandic ponies.

horses' needs. Nevertheless, at least the most common behavioural disturbances should be mentioned briefly as well as their connection with mistakes in keeping or handling.

Aggression against humans can be expressed as spontaneous attacks, biting, well-directed kicks or threats.

The reason is often uncertainty in rank, or a situation where the person is lower down the pecking order than the horse. Horses will bite and kick when they are frightened, and show aggressive behaviour when driven into a corner, whereas normally they would flee.

A dominant and aggressive horse is corrected through strict, consistent and fair basic education. When dealing with a "fear biter", identifying the cause of the pain and fear is most important.

Aggression against other horses is the result of mistakes in the horse's upbringing, when the young horse had neither the opportunity to practise species-specific communication, nor was able to find its own place between dominance and submission.

This form of aggression is also characterised by either fear or dominance. A long holiday in a herd may help, although this type of correction sometimes carries significant risks for all the horses involved and it is not always successful because the influential phases occur usually at a very early age.

Keeping the horse separately in an open stable can be a compromise.

Tying up problems can have very different causes. Being tied up away from other horses is an unusual and frightening experience for a young horse. Mistakes during this basic training, especially having to stand for too long and without supervision, or accidents (too long a rope, tied up too low) can lead to panic and undisciplined behaviour every time the horse is tied up.

Constant but gentle practice will correct this. The young horse has to learn to stand still and remain calm, but must not be exhausted by excessively long learning phases and isolation. It needs to learn that nothing untoward is going to happen to it. Impatient behaviour must not be punished; the horse should rather be praised when the desired behaviour is shown.

Biting the bars, or chewing, incessant licking, playing with the tongue or teeth grinding are actually behaviourisms linked to eating that become uncontrollable when the horse is not properly kept and fed.

Too little forage and too much hard feed can lead to an increased need for exercise. The confined horse will search for an outlet, and in the end release the tension through alternative actions. Radical changes of the feeding and stabling regime will help: plenty of fibre, hard feed suitable for required work, constant exercise and social contact. Some of these disturbances can lead to actual damage of the teeth (biting bars), but most are generally harmless, but are nevertheless a sign of incorrect stable management and feeding.

Bucking under the saddle happens when horses have a "knotted back", and can be caused by tension and pain. Lack of exercise (a resting day!) can also lead to violent bucking at any possible opportunity. In the wild, bucking and kicking are usually signs of joy or excessive energy. Most harmless bucks when the horse is going into canter can be explained that way too.

While a few bucks can be anticipated and tolerated, repeated bucking is a sign of more serious underlying problems that need to be investigated, not least because of the associated dangers.

The exercise regime, saddle, seat of the rider, stable management and feeding have to be checked. If the tension persists, the whole musculoskeletal system has to be examined.

Running off is a danger for both horse and rider, because a truly fleeing horse cannot be controlled. This is different from a fresh gallop that may be a bit faster than planned; here, the horse no longer reacts to any aids and runs off in a panic, regardless of the danger.

Horses that run off without any obvious reasons, going from pulling and not reacting to the bit to galloping off, are often encouraged by fleeing companions, or they run away

Fear, pain and fatigue are often the cause of problems under the saddle.

from a stressful situation. Depending on the way they behave, various solutions can be tried, all of which aim to regain the control by the rider. Horses running off without apparent reason respond to stimuli that cannot be influenced by the rider (mainly pain in the back or mouth), or they react in by panicking in situations that remind them of previous, negative experiences. Pulling horses are heavy on the bit and increase their speed gradually, shorten their strides or go sideways, react less and less to aids and end up racing. The reasons why are often the rider (hand, seat), tack (poorly fitting saddles, sharp bits), and also poor training (lack of discipline, fatigue, uncontrolled races).

Running off because of a logical flight reaction has to be understood as species-specific behaviour. The threshold for this stimulus, however, can be lowered by appropriate actions.

If horse and rider trust each other, and if the animal is not sheltered from environmental influences but is exposed to normal sights, sounds and smells during training, it will not lose its composure so easily.

Head shaking can have many different mental and physical causes:

Pulling horses need good training rather than a double bridle.

not all are known yet. Persistent head shaking is often triggered by a hard contact, wrong bits, teeth problems or the inappropriate use of side or draw reins. It is also known that an allergic reaction to sunlight, irritation of the optical nerve or infections in the head area can lead to constant head shaking.

Only a thorough examination of everything including the tack will reveal the reasons, but in some cases the causes remain unclear. Removal of the underlying cause, a fly mask or treatment with special medication, may help.

Strong male behaviour is a whole complex of male mannerisms, which is characterised mainly by increased aggression. This aggression can be directed against mares, humans or against the stallion himself ("auto mutilation"). Incorrect, isolated stabling and artificial breeding techniques lead to many further disturbances that are expressed in various ways. Some stallions have no libido, while others mount everything that cannot get out of the way quickly enough – even a person bending forward! Aggression towards people and other horses is such a big problem partly because even some breeders regard this behaviour as normal for a male animal, and therefore do not try to address it.

When kept properly, stallions only

show aggression towards mares and other horses during normal arguments, and some can even be particularly friendly towards people. Correctly brought up stallions are easier to train, they want to please people and build up a close bond with "their" person. And that is completely independent of their breed...

Clinging is a behavioural problem that is characterised by an exaggerated attachment to certain companions or to the stable, the whole herd or a familiar area. A clinging horse cannot be moved away from the herd or out of the box or stable, and will not be led or ridden to the school.

This behaviour is based on horses' need for close contact with their social partners. Only a trusting relationship with their keeper or rider enables horses to regard them as a substitute for the presence of other horses. The people on the other hand have to establish themselves as a leader whom the horse will follow, the way it would follow the dominant mare. Negative experiences when leaving the group (very early weaning, weakness or brutality when ridden) can exaggerate this problem.

Wind sucking is one of the best-known vices, where the horse suck a small amount of air into its oesophagus. The horse will either place its incisor teeth on an object (fence, door, other horses!) or wind suck freely. It was once believed that wind suckers would swallow large amounts of air and develop colic more often than other horses; it was also thought that wind sucking was

Riding with a driving bridle – no surprise that the big boy responds with head shaking!

"contagious", meaning other horses would copy the behaviour. Both are wrong. Wind sucking is a reaction to problems in stable management and exercise regime that can have various causes. A certain genetic predisposition is currently being considered. Unfortunately, wind sucking is a vice that becomes autonomous, i.e. that will continue even after improving the living conditions.

As this behavioural disturbance is basically harmless, dubious measures like operations, belts or wiring the whole surroundings should not be executed.

Circling, a movement shown predominantly in the box, is a stereotype behaviour, like weaving, that can occur in an unstimulating environment and can be avoided and treated with proper stable management.

Reasons for the *resistance to be tacked up* are more often encountered at the beginning of the training, when a horse is broken in too quikkly or is fatigued. Riding in a wrong and tense collection, or using the wrong saddle can lead to it. Resisting the saddle can be expressed by a reluct-ance to be tacked, also by rearing, bucking or not moving at all. The underlying cause has to be corrected first, for example a badly fitted saddle, pulling the girth too tight or insufficient warming up phases. Furthermore, the horse has to be slowly familiarised with being touched, with the saddle, the girth, mounting and riding.

Horses *shy* when exposed to sights, sounds or smells that frighten them. Shying is a normal reaction for a flight animal and not a vice, as long as stimulus and reaction are in proportion. Exaggerated shying, that can be expressed as eit-

her a frightened reaction to a minimal stimulus or a panic-stricken flight, disregarding any influence of the rider, can be caused by an isolated upbringing and keeping or distrust of humans. Horses, being inquisitive individuals, can be familiarised with numerous potentially hazardous environmental stimuli and can be controlled and calmed by their rider in dangerous situations. It would be wrong to shelter a spooky horse from environmental influences or to forcefully expose it to the cause of its fear. It will then automatically regard the trigger as negative, instead of overcoming its anxiety.

Rearing occurs in different situations and has various causes. When performed under the saddle, it is often a sign of a back problem, a badly fitted saddle or bit, insensitive hands or very short draw or side reins. Rearing in front of a person is mainly shown by aggressive stallions when the ranking order has not been established.

Weaving is another stereotype behaviour: the front legs are placed wide apart and the horse sways from one side to the other. It all repeats itself: the causes are mistakes in upbringing and stable management. As with crib biting, weaving does not seem to be a health hazard, nor is it usually copied by other horses, but contrary to crib biting an improvement of living conditions will normally lead to a complete cure.

All the best for your horse

Treatments of difficult behaviour are as variable as their symptoms. Prophylaxis, however, is far more successful than any corrective measures and it simply consists of proper upbringing and keeping of all horses. Only when a horse is allowed to be a horse, when it can express all its natural genetic mannerisms, will it not release the subsequent tension as abnormal behaviour. Species-specific stable management requires riders and owners to readjust: some have to let go of the belief that highly bred sports horses cannot be kept in an open stable and are fundamentally different from other, more native breeds; the defenders of open stable management on the other hand must not simplify the situation and be self-righteous when their own horses are standing in mud and droppings, and have to pick their hay out of a puddle of urine. Correct management requires genuine knowledge and honest compassion for our horses and it is therefore necessary to widen our own mental horizon beyond the bars of the stable.

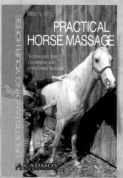

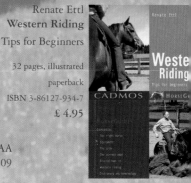